COVID-19

When Life Comes at You Fast

JOHN A. REAVES

Printed in the United States of America
ISBN: 978-1-7357030-3-9 (paperback)
ISBN: 978-1-7357030-4-6 (ebook)

Canoe Tree Press

4697 Main Street
Manchester Center, VT 05255

Canoe Tree Press is a division of DartFrog Books.

This book is dedicated to brave millions of Americans who selflessly put themselves in harm's way to keep our country running. This book is also dedicated to the 300M+ persons who lost their fight to COVID and the loved ones they left behind who must keep their memory alive. We will NEVER forget you.

CONTENTS

CONTENTS

INTRODUCTION

A voice is an instrument that most of us have and can choose to use however we see fit. Since I could remember, if a person asked me a question, I would respond with an answer or opinion. What generally caused discourse was how I answered the question. Like most people, throughout my life, I have been in situations where forces have attempted to silence my voice, whether it was an essay in school that struck a nerve with a teacher, leading them to grade the paper based on their feelings rather than its merits; in a professional setting where one is governed by hidden rules and protocols that tend to frown upon honest feedback and transparency; socially, when divergent views are quashed by harsh social media rebuke; or even under COVID-19, a dreadful disease that has forced most of us to rethink what we do with our time and minds when sequestered in our homes.

The serenity of space to think led me to write a series of essays on my life as a Black man, which culminated in my first book, *Will I Always Be A __ In America? A Black Man's Reflections on Living in America*. The book was released in the early fall of 2020. I thought I would take a break from writing and focus on promoting the book. After a month or so of not writing, I found myself longing to write more about my reflections, but with an emphasis on COVID-19. Hence, this book was born. This book is a collection of ten essays that capture my thoughts on everyday issues, including unemployment, isolation, faith, living with COVID, the vaccination debate, political civility, and other reflections that I thought would resonate with readers. The essays are quick reads that follow a similar pattern to those in my first book, share my thoughts with the reader, and welcome readers to my COVID-19 journey through self-reflection.

I wish I could turn back the clock and imagine what 2020 would be like without COVID-19. Before 2020, America struggled to find solutions to unemployment, racial disparity, homelessness, poverty, climate change, and other issues. COVID-19 has demanded quick answers for these problems but, from what I can see, COVID has a trajectory for management while these preexisting issues have to wait in a line becoming so long that even an optimist like me feels like time to solve these problems is running out. If there is a silver lining on the horizon, it could be the ingenuity, grit, determination, intellect, and financial investment that have been funneled to manage and eliminate COVID-19. I wish similar means could be used to address the persistent problems that existed before COVID.

COVID-19 WILL NOT STOP ME FROM WANTING WHAT I WANT

I want to be strapped to a ventilator to breathe because I refuse to wear a mask.

I want to stand over my loved one's casket because I am so hell-bent on having my family over for dinner that I am willing to risk exposing them.

I want to collect unemployment because I refuse to wash my hands consistently so that the virus won't shut down my company.

I want to live my life on my terms, and I will be damned if I will allow anyone to tell me how to live it.

I do not care about COVID-19 because it is just a virus, and the only people that die from it should have died.

Most people would read these statements and be outraged. Nevertheless, COVID-19 continues to invade our lives because of our choices. Choices that have turned COVID-19 into one of the ten most lethal viruses to invade earth.[1]

When I was a toddler, my mom told me not to touch the stove because it could harm me. On one auspicious occasion, she turned her head, and not only did I touch the stove, but I also managed to tip over a boiling pot of hot water all over my legs. Miraculously, I did not suffer any scarring or long-term deformities from the incident. I generally listened to my mom when she told me not to do something, but now and then, I ignored her and suffered the consequences. I appreciate my mom and other people with authority, knowledge, and wisdom, giving me advice that may protect me from harm, or worse, death. For instance, I remember the endless television and newspaper ads and family and friends advising me not to smoke, use drugs, or consume alcohol excessively. For me, the strong recommendations were effective because I never tried illegal drugs, although I did dabble with alcohol. One time in college, I attended a party and willingly participated in a series of beer bong rushes, where a funnel is attached to a long tube and beer is poured into the funnel until the person

---

1. Visual Capitalist, www.visualcapitalist.com/history-of-pandemics-deadliest/

says stop, or the person stops pouring it. I vaguely remember seeing eight beer cans being poured into the funnel. Before this, my alcohol consumption was minimal, and I'm not sure what possessed me to partake in this event, but I did. After crawling a quarter of a mile on my knees across campus to my dorm, I managed to climb into my loft bed and pass out. The next morning, I woke up to a room painted with vomit and a severe headache, which I now know to be a hangover headache. When I asked my roommate what happened, he told me he found me hanging from my bed. He tried to wake me up, but I did not respond. He went for a second opinion from a few of our neighbors, and they all indicated I would probably sleep it off.

When I think about this experience and all of the things that could have happened, I stop myself and focus on what I can prevent from happening in the future. Over thirty years later, I've never been that intoxicated again. In fact, in the past twenty years, I can count how many drinks I have had on two hands. I do not have a problem with alcohol, but I have a healthy respect for it and what it can do to a person if it is not consumed in moderation.

When I think about the state America is in

with COVID-19 and the sheer disregard for doing all we can to stop the spread of this virus, it reminds me of the advice I received about drugs and alcohol. I suspect the COVID-19 compliance problem is due to adults preferring to give advice rather than take it. As I am writing this, over 300k people in America have lost their lives because of COVID-19. The Centers for Disease Control and Prevention (CDC), White House Coronavirus Task Force, state government officials, and many other entities are pleading with American citizens to wear a mask, practice social distancing, and wash hands for at least twenty seconds.[2] Before writing this essay, I did not give considerable thought to how easy it is to disregard advice, even when it is a matter of life or death. For instance, I previously mentioned that I had never tried illegal drugs. The main reason is my fear of being arrested and going to jail. The other reason is I know many people who have died or now live dramatically altered life because of their use of drugs or alcohol. Some conditions brought on or aggravated by drug and alcohol use include kidney failure, cirrhosis of the liver,

---

2. Center for Disease Control and Prevention, www.CDC.gov

schizophrenia, various types of cancers, heart conditions—too many problems to list. Most of us know of a situation in which someone has succumbed to drugs or alcohol, but we often believe that somehow our family members—and even we—are exempt from it.

We can blame America's failure to combat, or at least manage, the virus on all three US government branches: the legislative, for not passing laws that would prevent people from being so selfish and self-centered; executive, for not executing laws that would help save us from ourselves; and judicial levels, for turning a blind eye to the negligence of both our legislative and executive branches. We can blame the service- and gig-workers for not having a job that allows them to work from home. We can blame doctors and nurses for not wearing enough protective gear to shield them from the virus. While all of these situations have a hand in spreading and fighting COVID-19, we must blame ourselves for the lack of progress we have made battling the virus if we must assign blame. Let's use the example of visiting a friend or relative. Based on the CDC's criteria, unless the friend or relative is in harm's way, what is the urgency? What about the gatherings where we have seen countless attendees contracting and sometimes even dying from the virus, but we still do what we want to do? What about the people who complain about others not following CDC guidelines and when they think no one is looking, go to an indoor restaurant with their friends, fly to see relatives, attend church or a public event with hundreds of people, or take off their masks when walking through a crowd of people? While there may not be a news camera or cell phone to police our actions, COVID-19 does not take a break, and it continues to infect and kill some without any warning.

My wish for America is to stop blaming everyone else for the state we are in fighting COVID-19 and for each of us to take action in the communities where we live. Oddly, we do not need the government or some notable person to tell us what to do. I would like the federal government's leadership, but that is an essay for another time. We know what to do, but we choose not to do it. None of us know when the COVID-19 slaughter will end. But we do know that the virus appears to thrive on our disregard to comply with the CDC. We do know that more people will needlessly lose their lives because we want what we want. For me, I am a terrible loser, and I hate that we are losing the COVID-19 battle. Maybe if we turned fighting COVID-19 into a game or sporting event that awarded prizes for keeping the infection rates down, people would be willing to comply with CDC standards. For me, the ultimate award for saving a human life should be enough. Whatever it takes to manage and eliminate COVID-19, count me in. Our reality is one person, or a few million persons will not win the COVID-19 fight. It will take all of us, all 300 million+, to get in the fight. The question becomes, do we as Americans want to fight, or do we want to be COVID-19 doormats that will only try to fight it when the virus arrives in our or a loved one's bodies?

TEACHING DOGS NEW TRICKS: WHEN CHANGE IS A MATTER OF LIFE OR DEATH

Much is made of a dog learning the rules and regulations to live with its owner. If the dog does not quickly learn key commands—sit, wait, down, come, etc.—the owner may solicit a dog trainer's help or give up and send the dog to an animal shelter. It is at the animal shelter where the dog could be euthanized if a suitable home is not available or deemed too old or classified as too wild to tame. Thank goodness that life for humans is not this cut and dry, at least in the United States. We are generally afforded the luxury of learning at our own pace, even when it infringes upon other people's rights. The First Amendment of the United States Constitution states, "Congress shall make no law respecting an establishment of religion, or prohibiting the free exercise thereof; or abridging the freedom of speech, or the press; or the right of the people peaceably to assemble, and to petition the Government for a redress of grievances."[3] This statement's challenge is it does not cover items such as hate speech, smoking in a public location, or flag burning. Whether or not the amendment should protect these acts rests in the hands of each American, but to date, and thanks to the current US Constitution, those acts are not protected.

COVID-19 has ushered in a new debate about whether it is the right of a person to not publicly wear a mask, social distance, and wash hands. The CDC has issued several mandates for Americans to engage in practices that may prevent contracting and spreading the virus, including all the aforementioned items. Regrettably, these practices have launched a firestone where the main political parties in America have politicized these protocols to where Americans are picking sides. America is the only industrial country where such disdain for employing safety practices that may save millions of lives has led people to cite the First Amendment as their defense. As painful as it is to plead with individuals who choose to exercise their constitutional right rather than save

---

3. First Amendment of the United States Constitution, https://constitution.congress.gov/constitution/amendment-1/

lives, including their own, it is their right. It is a stance I do not understand, but I will sadly respect. Using the example of the dog learning to conform to human rules, regardless of which side we take on this issue, just as a dog can be trained, humans can learn to adapt to change.

Before the onset of COVID-19 in the United States, we have not been known for our willingness to adapt to change. Places such as Japan, South Korea, and China have been wearing masks for decades. Some of the reasons include fighting diseases, pollution, and protecting image.[4] Oddly, another variable that contributes to how COVID-19 is viewed is the lack of a comprehensive policy that details how all Americans must govern themselves as it relates to the virus. Depending upon what part of the United States you reside in, the policy may be quite different. It is as if we live in fifty different countries. A silent but gallant contender in the lack of the US embracing change is how COVID-19 has impacted communities of color. Yes, Title VI of the Civil Rights Act of 1964 protects all Americans from discrimination based

4. Voice of America, https://www.voanews.com/science-health /coronavirus-outbreak/not-just-coronavirus-asians-have-worn-face- masks-decades

on race/sex/religion/creed. Still, similar to other societal ills, America's playbook has not changed when helping these communities fight COVID-19. They are fending for themselves. Yes, discrimination continues to rear its ugly head in the United States and will outrun COVID-19. Nevertheless, we cannot blame racism for COVID-19, but discrimination does factor into how we as a country tackle this dreadful virus.

COVID-19 does not discriminate when it comes to infecting its victims. Whether one becomes gravely ill or dies will depend on the person's immune system and its ability to fight off the virus. The CDC has indicated that 8 out of 10 COVID-19-related deaths reported in the United States have been among adults aged sixty-five years and older.[5] COVID-19 also appears to kill more men than women, which is why it is hard to comprehend why it is less likely for a man than a woman to adhere to the CDC guidelines. This may be painful information, but we must steer the course and practice behaviors that we want others to emulate.

As America waits for a full rollout of a vaccine, which will take months to become available to

---

5. Center for Disease Control and Prevention, CDC.gov

all Americans, we must do what we can to protect others and ourselves from COVID-19. Yes, this means wearing a mask, social distancing, vigorously washing our hands, and minimizing the frequency at which we leave our homes. It also means that we have to be open to new tricks, such as training our minds to accept that COVID-19 is a virus and does not have feelings, and is currently at the center of our universe. I do not know about you, but I am tired of seeing daily news clips of families who have lost several members because they did not take it seriously. Or health and service industry workers who have lost their lives because they were providing services vital to our survival. Or families whose children have fallen behind in school because they do not have the resources for remote learning or a tutor. While it is our right not to wear a mask, social distance, or wash our hands, it is also the right of these people to protect themselves and adhere to CDC protocols. The question becomes, whose life is worth saving—mine, yours, or all of our lives?

THE UBIQUITY OF COVID-19: HAVES AND HAVE-NOTS

Today I look out of my window, and it is sunny and about seventy degrees on this December day. The leaves are all nearly brown, but several yellow and red ones peek through the woods. Something that I cannot see but is lurking outside, and possibly inside, of my house, is COVID-19, a colorless, invisible virus that has proven to be more evasive than the flu and deadlier on a daily per-capita in the United States than heart disease and cancer.[6] What makes COVID-19 so ubiquitous is that it is also a terrorist, invading anyone it can get inside of, causing so much destruction that billions of dollars have been invested worldwide into solutions to manage and eventually eliminate it. What makes this terrorist different from any other type of terrorist is no matter where you live on earth, simply mentioning COVID-19

---

6. Healthleadersmedia.com, https://www.healthleadersmedia.com/covid-19/coronavirus-becomes-number-one-cause-death-day-us-surpassing-heart-disease-and-cancer

elicits fear, which is far more powerful and elusive than other terrorists.

COVID-19 not only causes physical and psychological destruction, but it also tends to be discriminatory, killing people above sixty-five and those with preexisting conditions such as high blood pressure, diabetes, cancer, heart conditions, obesity, and several others.[7] It also causes financial devastation, leaving millions of people in the United States collecting unemployment and overwhelming American food banks.

What COVID-19 has also managed to accomplish, unintentionally, is to expose the terrible job that America has done to eradicate poverty and homelessness. There should be a law against the US stock market rising to its highest levels since its inception, while record numbers of Americans cannot pay their rent and will be thrown onto the street. I do not have any issue with anyone profiting from the stock market's rise and fall, but how much money is too much? A simple definition of socialism is when property and natural resources (e.g., water, land, minerals) are owned publicly versus privately

---

7. Centers For Disease and Control Prevention, https://www.cdc.gov/coronavirus/2019-ncov/need-extra-precautions/people-with-medical-conditions.html

owned. I do not wish for America to become a system where there is no private ownership. However, when the top 1 percent of US households hold fifteen times more wealth than the bottom 50 percent combined,[8] one does begin to wonder if there is an economic system that does not leave millions of people wondering where they will get their next meal. A financial system that rewards ingenuity and hard work and is more forgiving if you have a misstep like lose a job or become ill and are no longer able to generate an income from a wage. COVID-19 did not cause this problem, but its reign has forced millions of Americans into a hole that deepens as the virus rages across the country.

It is exciting that several vaccines are on the horizon, and a few are being dispersed to slow down the virus's spread, hopefully. I would like to see complimentary vaccines that protect all Americans from poverty, homelessness, and racial disparity. The first vaccine would be designed to eliminate poverty and homelessness by simply providing a livable wage to any US adult over eighteen and a stipend for shelter. I'm sure some people are saying, "We already have food

8. CNBC, https://www.cnbc.com/2020/01/20/oxfam-worlds-billionaires-richer-than-a-combined-4point6-billion-people.html

stamps and Section 8 government programs," but what I am proposing is much more humane and designed to leave no person behind. As a nation, we have already dipped our toe toward this approach by giving most households a stimulus check. The second vaccine for racial justice would be to dispense by requiring all public and private companies' employees must be 35 percent people of color. Ten percent of this number must be executive leadership and board members. The penalty for non-compliance would be 35 percent of the public and private company's annual revenue. My question is: what is stopping America from finding the means to address these problems? I'm sure I speak for millions of people when I say that being healthy has its merits, but when you are hungry, homeless, and hopeless, an effective vaccine only scratches the surface.

People who have financial means and power (the Haves) are not shielded from the virus, but their risk can be managed by wearing a mask, social distancing, washing their hands, and minimizing unnecessary outings. In other words, contracting the virus is solely based on what they choose to do. The rest of the population (Have-Nots) do not have the luxury of barricading at home. Yes, they too must wear masks (if we can afford it or find someone to give us one), practice social distancing (if others around us are doing it), and wash our hands (if we have access to running water or hand-sanitizing fluids). In this case, providing for ourselves and our family is a necessity and not a choice. This is the America that we live in today. A place where a virus like COVID-19 widens the wealth gap by rewarding the Haves with bigger stock portfolios, access to unlimited COVID-19 testing, and numerous options to hire others to risk their lives to purchase and deliver their groceries and other life necessities—and even frills. Meanwhile, the Have-Nots can barely rub two pennies together to try their luck at the lotto; if they are fortunate to be able to work, they risk their lives and families' lives every time we leave the house and return home. The question I leave you with is: what or who will shoulder the blame for the state of poverty and homelessness in America once COVID-19 becomes a manageable virus?

WHY I BELIEVE IN GOD

COVID-19 has caused us to face many questions; for many, it has raised the ultimate question: *If there is a God, why does He allow so much death, suffering, and destruction from the virus?* COVID-19 will eventually pass, and how each of us navigate through this painful period in life or other challenges is up to each of us. It can be said there are three schools of thought when it comes to believing in God. One is that God is almighty, and He is the ruler of all things; another is that above the clouds and sun, there is nothing; and the third is somewhere in between the first two.

Whatever you choose to believe is personal, and how you choose to recognize your belief is up to you. I know the very thought that people can choose what they believe and how they believe will rub some the wrong way. Throughout history, thousands of people have lost their lives over what they believe; thus, understanding and respecting other views is important. I identify as a Christian and use the Bible as the compass for my life's journey. This pronouncement does not mean that I do not recognize many other religions and ways other people worship God. For me, I connect best with God through the practice of Christianity.

My belief in God began at an early age. Perhaps it resulted from my parents' influence, but as I began to experience life and the many good and painful encounters that it brought me, I learned to lean on God. Whether I was on the playground dealing with a bully, coping with the death of a parent, grandparents, and several other family members, or making decisions when confronted with several options that could have me in the hospital, jail, or casket, it was through reading the Bible and praying for direction that kept me moving forward. This laser focus was relatively easy until I went off to college.

I particularly remember my college days because it was in this climate that my belief in God was strengthened, while for most young adults, college is where thoughts and behaviors are questioned and formed. Like most college students, money was tight, temptation was high, and many people around me were making life look way too easy by using drugs, drinking alcohol, and choosing other negative outlets to get through this time. While I never doubted my belief in God, I was frustrated with my life because it felt like taking classes, working a job, and socializing with friends was so hard that I could not see the light at the end of the tunnel. For a few semesters, I could not muster a grade point average above a C+ while the people around me appeared to party all night, still get good grades, and have a never-ending supply of money. What I found interesting is when my peers did get themselves into a situation, they would resort to using drugs or alcohol to take the edge off of what life issues brought them. For me, it was praying to God for direction and inner peace. For me, this approach was much more fulfilling and safe than some of the other alternatives.

What I learned about my belief in God during my college years is the relationship is not transactional. Meaning, in exchange for staying away from drugs or not partying all night, I would receive money from scholarships and work during the school year and summers to pay for books and rent. What I learned instead was to be still and pray to God for strength and direction. It was this direction that provided me with hope and a clear mind to face life's challenges. My belief propels me today when I am faced with a difficult decision and feeling optimistic or frustrated about life. For me, God has been the only constant with whom I can have a conversation without feeling judged, belittled, or defeated because of what I have or have not done.

Some will read this essay and assert that I have somehow been brainwashed by a religious sect or am trying to convince people to believe in God. My message is similar to what I stated in the opening paragraph—my belief in God is personal. I share my belief because I hope it may help those who do not understand why some people believe in God and others do not.

The chorus to a hymn, "Blessed Assurance," resonates with me because it reflects the personal nature of my relationship with God:

This is my story, this is my song
Praising my Savior all the day long
This is my story, this is my song
Praising my Savior all the day long.[9]

---

9. Hymnary.com, p. 27

It was almost as if the writer, Fanny Crosby, encouraged each of us not to be afraid to tell our stories and not be scared to praise God.

Whatever your story may be, consider what approach you take to get through life. For me, it is believing in God and reading the Bible to help cope with the myriad of life issues that affront me. Just because I believe, I am not exonerated of pain, loss, and misery. I am, however, empowered to face my tomorrow by how I choose to get through it. I choose to believe in God, and the following chorus of the hymn "Because He Lives" by Bill Gaither captures my sentiments:

Because He lives, I can face tomorrow
Because He lives, all fear is gone
Because I know He holds the future
And life is worth the living, just because He lives[10]

There are so many approaches to answering why God allows death, sorrow, and destruction. For the record, I do not know. I wish I had an answer that would address this question. There are several references in the Bible that provide

10. Hymanary.com, p. 106

some context to this question, but does it truly spell out an answer? From my interpretation, the answer is no. For me, I do not dwell on the "why" or "what." I focus on what I can control and leave the rest up to Him. The new question becomes, what do you have to lose by believing in God? Last I checked, it is free.

LONELINESS, ISOLATION, AND COVID-19

Many of us are searching for an approach to soothe our minds when it comes to grappling with the possibility of contracting COVID-19. Popular methods for coping with this anxiety include seeking counsel from a licensed medical professional, indulging in alcohol or drugs, exercising, meditating, and conversing with a family member, friend, or colleague. However, individuals who do not have access to these methods or choose not to partake of such options may attempt to power through and subsequently find themselves alone. For some, this may be a matter of choice, while others may not have anyone they can reach out to. I instantly think of our senior citizens, the infirmed, or persons already living alone; however, loneliness and isolation are just as real for individuals residing in a house full of people.

Growing up, I had a large family and shared a home with my siblings and parents. While

I periodically played with my siblings, I frequently found myself feeling lonely and isolated. Other than my belief and faith in God, I did not feel I had a safe outlet to share my innermost thoughts or someone I could vent to without feeling judged or criticized. At times, my loneliness reverberated in self-despair. What I did not know until much later in life is that my siblings experienced similar feelings. As a kid and young adult, I discounted their feelings, which most of us tend to do when we are so consumed with our thoughts that we have no room to empathize with others. However, I had the great fortune to have a spouse who could see that my narrative of loneliness and isolation was similar to what she heard from my siblings. This revelation was a shock to my system, but with my wife's help, I was able to see my siblings' perspectives and apply what I had learned to help others.

Today, I enjoy a healthy support system that I do not take for granted, as I know these feelings of loneliness and isolation can resurface at any time. Therefore, each of us must look both within and outside of our respective bubbles and reach out to one another. One of the best approaches is in-person visits; while these visits may not be advisable under COVID-19, they may be necessary depending upon the circumstances. Complying with social distancing rules is important, but human touch has become as prized as winning the lottery for those who live alone. The Texas Medical Center published an article highlighting a condition called "touch starvation," which refers to the lack of physical contact between two living beings.[11] The article included a 2014 study conducted by Carnegie Mellon University, citing how hugs help our bodies fight off infections. The study asserts that our brains produce chemicals that help us feel less threatened and more at ease. While this does not mean that hugs can cure COVID-19, it may help the body deal with this disease's trauma. In Carnegie Mellon's study, "406 participants responded to questionnaires and telephone interviews to evaluate their level of social support and frequency of hugs over the course of fourteen consecutive evenings. After researchers intentionally exposed the participants to the cold virus to test their immune functions, they found that 'those who receive more hugs are somewhat protected from infection

---

11. Texas Medical Center, https://www.tmc.edu/news/2020/05/touch-starvation/

and illness-related symptoms' and 'physical contact with a close other [reduces] the effects of stress on biological markers thought to be precursors of disease.'"[12] Outside of exchanging physical touch, we can exercise the power of a warm voice, which carries little risk if you are six feet away from the person. Video chats and warm phone calls carry no risk but certainly do not replace the human touch. Nevertheless, how do you hug someone without contracting or transmitting the disease? There are several ways to accomplish this goal, but I encourage you to seek a medical professional's advice.

When I wake up every morning, I look out the window to see the weather. Is it rainy? Cold? Sunny? Depending upon where you live, the weather can be all three simultaneously. However, while we can observe the weather, we cannot see COVID and what destruction it may bring for the day. We all hope for an end to COVID-19's reign, but we need to learn to live with it so long as it is in the atmosphere. We cannot control who COVID infects, but we can control how we interact with one another.

Amid the darkness and despair, I see a bright

---

12. Texas Medical Center, https://www.tmc.edu/news/2020/05/touch-starvation/

light at the end of the tunnel. I wish we could skip the COVID journey and arrive at this bright light, but we must walk through the tunnel, day by day until COVID is managed. Oliver Goldsmith, a 7th-century novelist and playwright, stated, "Life is a journey that must be traveled no matter how bad the roads and accommodations."[13]

As we continue to embark on the COVID journey, we must reach out to our loved ones, friends, colleagues, and strangers. Loneliness and isolation are real, but, unlike COVID, humanity can prevail so long as we each reach out and touch one another.

---

13. Quotenova.com, https://www.quotenova.net/authors/oliver-goldsmith /qw3gkk

WHEN THE PHONE DOES NOT RING

It is hard to believe that over a decade ago, I wrote an essay regarding an aspect of the job search that can feel almost as painful as being unemployed—when the phone does not ring. In the advent of text, social media, and emails, there are numerous ways to receive word of an interview or job offer, but the preferred medium for most still appears to be the telephone, or should we say, "cell" phone.

Regardless of the industry, searching for a job can be difficult, but add COVID-19 and a record number of job layoffs into the mix, securing employment just went from "challenging" to almost impossible. How many of us have sent out hundreds of résumés and not received one phone call in return? How many of us have received an email from a recruiter expressing interest but no actual phone call to set up an interview? How about receiving an interview and nailing it (at least you thought you did), only to receive a thanks-but-no-thanks email two months later? For those who are unemployed, work gigs, or planning a career change, waiting for the phone to ring can be gut-wrenching, but it does not have to be.

When the phone does not ring, many thoughts assault our minds, such as, "How do I provide for my family?" or "How will I keep my home?" These events may appear to be uncontrollable, but one thing we can control is our point of view. Sometimes, only a change of perspective is needed to get those creative juices flowing, leading to a new opportunity. I know the last thing anyone wants to read or hear is changing your attitude somehow can help with a job search, but in the end, it is up to each of us to create a narrative that propels us beyond our current state of mind.

For instance, let us say you lose your job and can receive unemployment, but it barely provides enough to pay essential bills. An approach is to start to think about your other options. Yes, you have options—maybe you just have not taken the time to think through them. Again, I understand the electric and phone bills are due, but as you try to find ways to pay these essential bills, you must also begin to invest in yourself. My go-to method is to write. Writing provides an outlet for me to share my experiences with others and capture what I feel at a particular moment in time. It also enables me to organize my thoughts to let others (a counselor, family member, friend, or former co-worker) know what I am feeling and possibly how they can provide support and assistance. For you, it might be turning one of your hobbies into a money-generating opportunity or attempting to find success in a business or field that may not have been available to you before because of your previous work commitments.

Another option that most people do not consider when unemployed is to volunteer. Amid our current storm of not having a job, many other people may only have a few days to live because of a deadly virus or have a debilitating illness that does not allow them to hold a job. Volunteering can accomplish two goals: first, you can help someone else, and second, it provides you with an escape from your current situation. A bonus is you have no idea who you will meet while volunteering.

One more way to look at this is that you have a clean slate to do whatever you want to do with your time to generate a legal income. Yes, it may require some financial capital to begin, but there is absolutely nothing—but you—stopping you from starting something new. One of my favorite personal quotes is, "The only thing that is holding you back is what you see in the mirror."

The "waiting game" is not new for most of us. We have all likely applied for jobs in the past or been in a situation where we must wait for an answer after visiting a doctor, applying for a mortgage, filing an insurance claim, or participating in a host of life events. Though the circumstances vary, the outcomes are similar—we wait for the unknown.

It is no secret that finding a job during a recession is daunting, but it is not impossible. Keep a positive attitude and consider adopting a daily routine that allows you to perform a task at the same time every day. Some examples include exercising, walking, meditating, or reading a chapter of a book. When choosing an activity, consider turning off your phone. One of my favorite coping mechanisms for a non-ringing phone is to use the power of *dreaming*. Langston Hughes stated, "Hold fast to dreams, for if dreams die, life is a broken-winged bird that cannot fly." The same principle can be applied to your job search. Take this time to reinvent yourself. When you do find the new you, you may find that you have created the new you.

COVID-19 has forced many of us to apply survival skills we did not know we possessed. While we may not know when COVID-19 will end or when we will get our next jobs, what we do know is regardless of whether or not the phone rings, we must live for another day. A phone call with a job offer may improve how we choose to live, but it should not dictate why we live.

DYING TO WORK

What I like about US elections is that—regardless of your politics—*change will occur*. The challenge then becomes *what kind* of change? Like most Americans, to find the answer, we must wait for the dust to settle and for returning—as well as newly elected—leaders to be sworn into office. As we put the 2020 elections behind us, many Americans will now zoom in on which campaign promises will become realities transformed into actions:

- A solution that manages and potentially eradicates COVID-19.
- A solution that puts millions of Americans back to work and provides them with livable wages to buy food, housing, and possibly health insurance.
- A solution to advance racial justice and eliminate the ugly rhetoric that continues to plague America.
- A solution to reverse the climate change collision course that is no longer isolated

along the west and gulf coasts of the United States.

I recently joined millions of Americans in the unemployment line after my contract ended and was not renewed. This is the rugged terrain that most who work under contracts face, and, from time to time, we must secure new opportunities. However, during COVID, securing the next opportunity raised the bar to a level that even people like me who are highly educated and experienced are having difficulty clearing.

As I searched for new opportunities, I did not think I would have to ask myself this question: Would I accept a job that put me in danger of contracting and dying from COVID-19? Of course, I knew when my contract ended, but given the tight job market, do I now have to seriously consider jobs that require me to go into an office that has ignored all of the safety protocols the CDC?

Unfortunately, millions of Americans are not asking themselves this question. Instead, they are forging ahead because they need to pay their overdue rent and buy food for their families. The more than 270k people who have lost their lives to COVID-19 is a *real* number, and not providing for one's family is a real problem.

No one should have to choose between living or dying—but that's where we are as a nation.

The employed are not exempted from making a similar choice as those who are unemployed. When I think about firefighters, police officers, health professionals, transportation and hospitality industries, and others, all of these persons can choose to stay home or go to work and face the probability of contracting COVID-19. In many cases, the consequences may be forgoing paying their rents, mortgages, and feeding their families. Even for the employed, this is an awful choice they too have to make—stay safe or take the risk every day that may end in the loss of their life.

Prior to my contract ending, for months—yes, months—I have been working my networks and sending out hundreds of résumés for job opportunities. Recently, I was invited in for two in-person interviews. The first interview went relatively well, and most of the people I met were wearing masks, except for the company president. When one of my interviewers took me around the office to meet a few of the team members, I was surprised—*no one was wearing a mask, and everyone was close to each other.* I also noticed that at least five people had

jammed themselves into the president's office—
*no one was wearing a mask, and everyone was in
close proximity to each other.* A thought I had as
I watched these people in the crammed office
was if they had a say in whether they could wear
a mask without feeling some type of isolation or
retribution from their president or peers.

The second interview was different. When
I walked through the front door, I was taken
into a small conference room where no one
wore a mask. Instead of taking a seat and taking a chance, I made a beeline for the door. I
learned from both experiences that too many
people are not taking the CDC protocols seriously, despite the high COVID-19 infection rate
and deaths. What I will never understand is why
some people only acknowledge tragedy when
they are impacted by it. The controversy about
wearing a mask is preposterous because scientists have made it clear that masks save lives.
Japan and South Korea have worn masks for
decades. Perhaps this may explain why these
countries' COVID-19 contraction and fatality
rates are much lower than America's.

I remember back in the mid-1980s when
people smoked in the workplace with little or
no regard to the proven fact that secondhand

smoke was killing millions of Americans. This practice—the right to smoke in the workplace—eventually ended, but it took way too long for nonsmoking to become universal. I believe that *to wear or not to wear a mask* is a personal right today, but it must become a nationwide requirement. Why? Because many of us do not have the luxury of deep bank accounts and other resources that allow us to choose. Perhaps a compromise is for companies that do not choose to honor the CDC protocols to let people know their mask policy until legislation is passed that orders *all* businesses, regardless of type, to adhere to the mask policy. Just as legislation mandated wearing seat belts and not smoking cigarettes indoors, we need a similar *mandatory policy on wearing masks—now a matter of life or death.*

SACRIFICE FOR THE
GREATER GOOD: COVID-19
VACCINE VOLUNTEER

I was watching the evening news when I saw a story about a virus that was spreading like wildfire in a small province in Wuhan, China. Unlike most wildfires, this virus was killing thousands of people without any warning. The virus was identified as the *coronavirus* disease (COVID-19), an infectious disease caused by a newly discovered *coronavirus*.[14] It's referred to as COVID-19, where "CO" stands for "corona," "VI" for "virus," and "D" for disease.[15] According to the World Health Organization, there are many types of human coronaviruses, including some that commonly cause mild upper-respiratory tract illnesses. COVID-19 manifests like its peer viruses but quickly turns into a disease that leaves debilitating illness or death for some.

---

14. Centers for Disease Control and Prevention (CDC), www.cdc.gov/coronavirus/2019-ncov/index.html
15. World Health Organization (WHO), www.who.int/emergencies/diseases/novel-coronavirus-2019

Like many Americans, I paused but felt confident this disease would not invade the United States, as it was attacking Wuhan, China. A few weeks later, COVID-19 had made its rounds to Europe, killing at least one thousand citizens daily in Italy. By this time, I was beginning to become concerned but still optimistic. Surely, the disease would stay abroad and not attack the United States. Days later, the first person in the United States was diagnosed with COVID-19, followed by several deaths in a Washington state nursing home. COVID-19 was in the United States and was quickly spreading across the country. Days later, the United States closed its borders and temporarily shut down the country. Fast forward to November 2020, where hundreds of thousands of people in the United States have lost their lives to COVID-19 with no end in sight.

If there is such a thing amid this dreadful virus, a ray of hope is the possibility of a vaccine, similar to what is used to manage seasonal flu and other viruses, such as pneumonia, shingles, hepatitis, etc. Several vaccines are on the horizon, with the strong potential of their first distribution occurring toward the end of 2020. This is welcome news for those who will take the vaccine and those who will forgo it. From what I understand from scientists, at least 60 percent of the US population must receive the vaccine before it can minimize the infection rate for persons who chose not to take the virus. The challenge is how many of the US population will be willing to take the vaccine. Polls have indicated that as many as 58 percent of those asked would receive a vaccine, but in reality, we have no idea of the number until the vaccines are readily available.

According to the Mayo Clinic, herd immunity occurs when a large portion of a community (the herd) becomes immune to a disease, making the spread of disease from person to person unlikely. As a result, the whole community becomes protected—not just those who are immune.[16] Oddly, herd immunity may have worked with other viruses such as polio, measles, chickenpox, etc., but the science does not back up that herd immunity will work for COVID-19.

When I heard about the vaccines and the stage-three trial process required before it can be approved for public distribution, I

16. Mayo Clinic, www.mayoclinic.org/diseases-conditions/coronavirus/in-depth/herd-immunity-and-coronavirus/art-20486808

started to think about whether or not I would accept the vaccine if it were to become available. Based on the information provided by the World Economic Forum, a typical vaccine takes ten years to successfully travel from the lab to the arm of a patient.[17] I also thought about the rapid innovations in science and technology that have made the reality of a vaccine possible in such a short period. Another thought that raced through my mind was the efficacy of the trials and whether people of color, like myself, would be turned away or allowed to participate but potentially suffer the same fate as the hundreds of Black men who were part of the 1932 Tuskegee Study of Untreated Syphilis in the Negro Male.

This experiment was supposed to take six months but spanned over forty years. About six hundred men from Alabama took part in the research. Two hundred of them were allowed to suffer the disease and its side effects without treatment, even after penicillin was discovered to cure syphilis.[18] The overall genesis of this

---

17. World Economic Forum, https://www.weforum.org/agenda/2020/06/vaccine-development-barriers-coronavirus/
18. Centers for Disease Control and Prevention - www.cdc.gov/tuskegee/timeline.htm

failed study was that participants did not provide their informed consent—the process in which a healthcare professional educates the patient on the risks and benefits of a procedure.[19] With all of these concerns swimming in my mind, I also asked my wife her thoughts on accepting the vaccine once it was available, and she indicated that she would like to do a wait-and-see before moving forward. I agreed with her but wanted to find out more about the Phase III trial study.

It was not long after my conversation with my wife that I received a phone call from my doctor's office asking me to participate in one of the drug trials. They emphasized the dire need of people of color to participate because the drug company truly wanted a diverse population to engage in the drug trial. Without any hesitation, I said yes, and a day later, I was filling out paperwork, undergoing an abbreviated physical, having bloodwork done, and being administered my first shot. An important detail that I was told when consenting to participate was that the study would last for two years, and I would not be told if I received the placebo or the vaccine. The visits were followed up with

19. The American Medical Association - https://www.ama-assn.org/delivering-care/ethics/informed-consent

several phone calls, and I kept an electronic diary. Oddly, I did not have any reaction from the initial shot and, surprisingly, no anxiety about participating in the trial. What I did not do, which was completely crazy, was inform my wife I was participating in the study. Why? I thought it would be best to get through the study successfully and then tell her about it. This was a ridiculous decision, but I suspected she would have had a problem with me participating in the study.

A month later, I received my second shot, and unlike the first shot, the second shot felt a little different. I could not put my finger on it, but when I got home, my arm felt like I had dipped it in cement and let it dry. I immediately took two Tylenol and placed an ice pack on it. I had some swelling, but I was still functional and able to work. The next day, the pain had subsided, and I did not have to take the Tylenol. I did not give it much more thought until I received weekly phone calls from the doctor checking my progress. To date, I do not know what I received, but it certainly did not feel like a saline solution, the ingredients of the placebo.

After a month or so had passed, I decided to alert my wife about what I had done and why it was important for me to participate in the trial. When I sat her down, instead of beating around the bush, I blurted out that I had joined the vaccine trial. She looked at me in horror but then asked me why I had not shared this information before deciding to participate. I stated that I did not believe she would have approved, and I thought if I got past the first month without any problems, she would be okay with it. My wife was concerned, but she did allow me to share why I thought it was okay to risk my life to participate in the drug trial. At the time of our conversation, over 210,000 people had already died from COVID-19, with a significant percentage of the deceased being people of color. I also shared with her thousands of people work on the firing lines with the high potential of catching and possibly dying from this disease. The final shove that pushed me over the edge to participate in the drug trial was when I heard the news stories of children losing both of their parents to COVID-19. I understood the risk and hoped that my family would appreciate me thinking of the hundreds of children that lost their parents to COVID-19—and that if this research was completed sooner, their parents might still be with us today.

I do have regrets about not sharing with my wife, kids, or family members my decision to participate in the vaccine drug trial before signing on the dotted line. I do not regret participating in the study and truly hope that my participation will help save millions of lives.

While writing this essay, the drug trial I participated in was unblinded, which means all vaccine trial participants know who gets what kind of treatment. My initial thoughts were confirmed that I had indeed received the vaccine. While the confirmation was great, I did not have any other emotions because the medical community has not determined how long the vaccine will last, whether I will need a booster shot, or if the shot will be a yearly event, similar to the flu shot. For many, being vaccinated may translate to resuming life as they knew it by gathering with crowds of people, taking vacations inside and outside of the United States, and simply breathing a sigh of relief. As the medical community addresses this question, I will continue to wear a mask, social distance, wash my hands, and minimize unnecessary trips. I will also encourage everyone within my sphere to get the shot and continue taking precautions until COVID-19 is under control.

I do have regrets about not sharing with my

wife, kids, or family members my decision to participate in the vaccine drug trial before signing on the dotted line. I also have regrets that I did not try harder to persuade other people of color to participate in the drug trial. I contacted a few close friends, and while none of them told me that I was crazy, they took the stance of my wife and said they would "wait and see." The waiting is what confirmed their decision to not participate because of the long line they will have to stand in to get the vaccine now that it is available. I do not regret participating in the study and truly hope that my participation will help save millions of lives, especially people of color who are often overlooked by medical scientists or too afraid to participate in a drug trial because of too many true events that harmed or killed people of color. I hope the overall positive outcome of the COVID-19 vaccine, the technology used to create it, and the thousands of volunteers who lend their lives to actualize the research will provide a path for people of color to actively participate in future drug trials.

CIVILITY WILL WIN

From September through November 3, 2020, Americans exercised their constitutional right to vote by casting a ballot to determine what kind of country they want to live in and who should govern it. November 3, 2020, has come and gone, and we have a winner of our presidential race and other national, state, and local elections. Now, the hard part is doing the job.

There is no shortage of problems that Americans look to our elected leaders to solve. Most have been on political dockets for decades, including global warming, racial respect and justice for Black and brown citizens, livable wages to allow millions of Americans to live above the poverty line, and health insurance that does not require some families to choose between filling their prescription or buying food. The latest entry that has been thrust to the top of the list is COVID-19. Over 300k Americans have died from this disease, and based on projections from several leading scientists, this number could reach 400k by the end of 2020.

The election results will not magically fix any of these problems but depending upon two factors, wealth—how much money and influence you have—and race—how society sees you versus how you identify yourself—will determine how Americans deal with the outcome of the November 2020 election and the growing list of complex issues. Naturally, other factors can be added to the mix, such as political affiliation, education, geographic location, and religion. These considerations further divide us as a country, but they do not have to. Divergent views are the supposition that we as Americans once celebrated, but now, those contrasting views have made us vilify each other. Now that the election is over, we must remember that we all have a hand in how we choose to govern ourselves.

What bothers me about election season is it takes on some of the not-so-great attributes of a large sporting event. Fans (or in this instance, political parties) take sides and cheer for their people to win, sometimes refusing to accept defeat when the scoreboard (in this case, votes) casts the winner. A notable difference between the two is skill, teamwork, and strategy rule the game. Certainly, money plays a factor in professional sports, but each player generally must have a level of skill to play the game. Politics, on the other hand, has some significant differences. Skill is not necessarily a requirement to win, and winners are less often elected because they have the best ideas. Money plays a significant role in elections because it enables political candidates to present their messages to prospective voters. Name recognition also helps, and exposing the candidate through media generally produces optimal results. Can you imagine if sporting games were decided by who had the best commercial? I cannot, and I pray I never have to. If we must think of our elections as a large sporting event, one major thing I wish future political events would possess is that all participants must meet certain prerequisites. Some of these requirements include: 1) Mental fitness or competency; 2) Pass a test that demonstrates an understanding of domestic and global issues, and that includes the ability to name states and capitals of fifty states and one hundred countries; 3) Bar anyone who runs for office that generates above $1M in annual dividends and interest. The goal here is to minimize people who run for office who are so far removed from understanding the daily grime of what the typical American family needs to provide for their families. We can debate what these skills must be, but I believe we all can agree that intellectual competency and a command of the basic tasks to perform in the role must be requirements.

My hope is we as Americans will chart a new course by saying no to transactional elitism and become advocates of civility with no tolerance for anything that gets in the way of common decency and respect for human life. I hope we hold all elective officials accountable for their actions, stop blindly endorsing policies that extend poverty, expand the racial divide, and ignite a sense of hopelessness that draws some to violence or substance abuse to cope. I hope that we restore laughter without using each other as targets.

An American author, George Santayana, famously said, "Those who cannot remember the past are condemned to repeat it." The litany of terror and trauma of 2020 will not instantly go away, but I am hopeful that newly elected political leaders will make it their mission to spend most of their time executing what they said they would do during their campaigns. I truly hope we all remember that we may not be able to control election outcomes, but we can control how we respond and treat one another. I genuinely hope we as Americans have all learned from 2020 and that our actions will prevent us from extending the terrors and traumas of 2020 into 2021 and beyond.

GRIEVING FOR NORMALITY
TO RETURN

For over thirty years, rain, sleet, or shine, I started my day at a gym. It did not matter where I lived or where I worked; going to the gym was a mainstay for me. On March 7, 2020, all that changed; the gym where I lived shut down to slow the COVID-19 spread. Little did anyone know that the gym and many other businesses would remain closed for months. Reality sunk in fast for me. I woke up the next morning as usual and began to get ready to head to the gym. When I went to grab my gym bag, I could not find it. I usually put it on a chair near the door with my keys, but it was not there. A few moments later, I realized I had buried it in a storage closet because I would not need it for a while. After pausing for a moment, I began to ponder what I would do about working out. For the record, I generally run outside when the weather permits, so half of my workout routine was virtually the same. The only adjustment I had to make was to run in the neighborhood versus running on the trail near the gym because it was temporarily shut down. That left planning my workouts to incorporate weight training and yoga. Because my head was pounding with frustration, I decided to go for a run and chart my course for the rest of my workout after that. A few hours later, I realized that I could move some items in our rec room, serving as storage as we updated the kitchen and other rooms. After discovering several YouTube yoga videos and countless workout videos, I plotted out what would be my new normal.

Nine months or so in, I have to admit that my workouts are so much better than when I went to the gym because I am working body parts that I seldom worked, and I learned to lift less weight and perform a multitude of exercises that worked most body parts, which cuts down on muscle strain. I elected not to return to the gym until COVID-19 is managed, and while all is well, I truly miss leaving the house and see-ing different people. While my socialization at the gym was confined to saying hello to familiar faces and occasionally joining a light-hearted conversation, the routine is what I miss most. I will return to the gym one day, but I am pleasantly surprised at how quickly I adapted to my new routine. I suppose being healthy and minimizing my chances of contracting the virus trumps going to a place that increases my exposure to COVID-19.

As the world awaits vaccines and other measures to curb and manage COVID-19, many of us want to return to doing what we did before the virus's onset. There is nothing wrong with craving normalcy, but when it involves doing what we have always done, perhaps using this time to switch things up instead of thinking about what we cannot do or where we cannot go opens us to endless possibilities. As children, we learn the importance of being nimble and adapting to new situations, but in some ways, as adults, we prefer to be stuck in our ways. In the book In the Fault in Our Stars, the author, John Green, states, "Grief does not change you, Hazel. It reveals you."[20] COVID-19 has caused so much darkness that it may take a lifetime to heal. It has also revealed some ugly behaviors such as political polarization, elitism, racial injustice, disregard for the homeless and jobless that we should let die with the virus. What I hope it has done for each of us is allow us to

---

20. John Green quote, https://www.goodreads.com/quotes/tag/john-green

reflect upon what things we will do differently once COVID-19 has ended and how doing some things differently will help someone else—and even ourselves—in the process.

I grieve for the millions who have contracted COVID-19. I grieve for the three-hundred thousand people in America who have died from COVID-19. I grieve for the millions of professionals who put their lives and their families' lives on the line to assist others. I do not grieve for returning to a routine that promotes complacency and little regard for others. Isaac Newton, a renowned physicist, affirms, "I have three things to teach: simplicity, patience, compassion."[21] This pandemic has changed all of us somehow, and maybe the solution to eliminating COVID-19 rests with simplifying our lives and practicing patience and deliberate compassion for others. COVID-19 is a killer, but that does not mean we need to be.

---

21. Isaac Newton quote, https://www.goodreads.com/quotes/tag/isaac-newton

ABOUT THE AUTHOR

John A. Reaves is a native of Washington, DC but considers Charlotte, NC his second home. He has lived in 8 states and has been employed with several Fortune 100 Multinational companies in several leadership capacities. He is married to Denise and has three adult children, Francis, Kayla, and Micah. He currently resides in Matthews, NC, a suburb of Charlotte. John is an avid fitness enthusiast, voracious reader, and writer.

ALSO BY JOHN A. REAVES

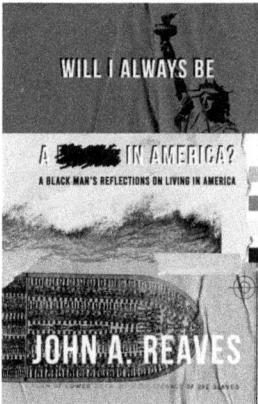

Will I Always Be A __ In America? A Black Man's Reflections On Living In America
This collection of ten essays reflects on the issues faced by people of color and offers recommendations towards solving racial inequality in society. Essay titles include "We Want to Live," "My First Confrontation with a Police Officer: Three Decades Later, I Cannot Forget It," and "The Neighborhoods I Live and Run Through: Are They a Symbol of Optimism or a Death Trap?" Every essay ends with a question to answer, encouraging thought and introspection from readers of all backgrounds.

Available on Amazon at
https://www.amazon.com/dp/B08JZGDSQZ
or **johnareaves.com**

www.ingramcontent.com/pod-product-compliance
Lightning Source LLC
Chambersburg PA
CBHW071122030426
42336CB00013BA/2171

9 781735 703039